Holiday Diet Cookbook

How to Survive the Holidays
(and Never Break Your Diet)

Dorothy R. Bates

Edited by Neal D. Barnard, M.D.

ISBN 1-882330-04-8
© 1994 Dorothy R. Bates
All rights reserved.
Published in the United States by The Magni Group, Inc.
P.O. Box 849 McKinney TX 75069
Printed in the United States of America.

Contents

Introduction

There are certain times of year when friends and loved ones gather together to celebrate a holiday. The mood is joyous, the food is usually fattening. How does someone who is watching his weight survive holidays and special occasions? You want to join in the festivities but not go all the way off your diet. This book has been created to show that you **can** plan, prepare, serve and enjoy most of the traditional holiday foods without destroying your diet, your figure and your health. Here are menus, recipes and techniques that will help you do it, a survivor's guide to holiday and party dining.

We have developed healthier versions of traditional holiday recipes so that you can eat favorite dishes without feeling guilty. Millions of Americans are making meals meatless, partly for health reasons, partly to make a statement about ecology and caring for the planet. Most cooks are avoiding fattening ingredients. Food can still be flavorful when fat is reduced. We can still enjoy mouth watering desserts.

Eating a varied and balanced diet is essential to maintaining good health. These recipes have *no cholesterol* - just as your doctor ordered. He or she may have suggested you reduce the amount of salt in your diet, also. Always taste before adding salt to a recipe.

The key to weight loss and weight maintenance is keeping one's daily fat intake low and eating more complex carbohydrates like fruits and vegetables, rice, pasta, and beans. It's important to avoid the saturated fats that clog arteries as much as possible. It is easy to tell which fats are saturated because they stay solid at room temperature. When you use canola or olive oil in cooking instead of old fashioned fats like lard and butter, you greatly reduce the amount of saturated fat and cholesterol in recipes. But all fats are fattening, even the reduced calorie margarines, so the recipes kindest to your health are those low in any kind of fat. If you wish to include bread and rolls in a meal,choose low fat ones and serve an all fruit jam or jelly instead of a fattening spread.

One of the exciting adventures that awaits you as you try new recipes and new products is a visit to a natural foods or health food store, the kind of store that has dozens of kinds of grains and beans, pastas and soy products. You can purchase a variety of legumes or grains in bulk as well as in packages. Purchase small amounts to try. In most natural foods stores you'll see big jars of spices and herbs and you can buy an ounce of this or an ounce of that at much lower prices than at a supermarket. If you buy dried herbs and spices in small amounts, and replace them frequently, they will always be full of flavor.

You will find TVP (textured vegetable protein), a de-fatted soybean product. It is such a good substitute for hamburger it is being used by pizza parlors and by the makers of many packaged foods. Try it in some of your recipes that call for ground meat. You will also find tempeh, a cultured soy product that has been a staple protein in Asian diets for years. You'll find all kinds of soy milks and several kinds of tofu. Most metropolitan areas boast one or more health food stores where grocery shopping can be a pleasure as well as an educational experience. Browse in the vegetarian cook book section for recipe ideas.

What can you do if this kind of natural foods store is not in your area? There may be a Food Buying Club you can join, where a group gets together to pool their orders and thus take advantage of bulk prices from a regional cooperative buying outlet. A farmer growning organic produce in your area may know of a group you can join. Many products can be ordered by mail.

Ingredients

Agar (also called **Kanten**) is a freeze dried sea vegetable that can be used like gelatin. It is calorie free, available in flakes or bars.

Broth: instead of canned soups, a good low sodium broth is made by simmering for about 40 minutes 4 cups of cut up vegetables in 6 cups of water. Use onion, carrot, celery, lettuce, turnip, parsley and a bay leaf. Cool and strain.

Carob is a natural low fat substitute for chocolate. It is made from pods of locust trees and has no theobromine. It's available as powder or chips.

Cream Cheese: use the low fat variety made from soymilk or tofu.

Eggs: a powdered egg replacer product for baked goods is available at health food stores. Follow package directions.

Fats: for frying and baking, use nonstick olive oil sprays; cook with nonstick pans and baking sheets.

Gluten or Seitan: also called Wheat Meat" is the protein part of wheat flour. It is available plain or flavored in health food stores, just mix with liquid and simmer in broth to prepare a chewy, high protein main dish.

Mayonnaise: reduced calorie, eggless mayonnaise is available. Or try some of the fat-free salad dressings.

Nutritional Yeast: use only the good tasting yellow flakes that are grown on a molasses base, *saccharomyces cerevisiae*. Good source of B vitamins.

Salt: reduce the amount of salt in recipes by using

herbs and spices for flavor. Read labels on cans and packages carefully for sodium content.

Sour Cream: use nonfat soy yogurt or low calorie sour cream made from tofu.

Soy Sauce: you can reduce sodium by mixing half and half with water to make two bottles out of one. Check label to avoid added preservatives or coloring.

Soy Yogurt can be used instead of dairy yogurt.

Sugar: try to use less, or substitute concentrated fruit juices like frozen unsweetened apple juice.

Tempeh: a cultured food made from soybeans, sometimes with both grains and soybeans. It has a nutty flavor, has no cholesterol, is rich in protein, vitamins, niacin and iron.

Tofu is a highly nutritious food made from soy milk.

Whipped Topping: non dairy toppings may contain tropical oils, read the label. It is easy to make a tasty topping with tofu.

List of Recipes

Appetizers and Starters

Beverages

Main Dishes

Side Dishes and Sauces

Baked Beans 57
Barbecue Sauce 55
Cornbread Dressing 74
Cranberry Orange Relish 18
Dressing 15
Gravy 16
Golden Gravy 75
Mexican Rice Casserole 42
Rice Pilaf with Mushrooms 62
Shiitake Sauce 28
Teriyaki Sauce 61

Salads

Coleslaw 63
Cucumber Dill Salad 64
Marinated Vegetables 41
Melon Rings with Yogurt 36
Potato Salad 56
Three Bean Salad 29
Tomato Aspic 24
Two Green Salad 70
Waldorf Salad 18

Vegetables

Acorn Squash Rings 83
Asparagus 23
Baked Onions 78
Broccoli with Sesame Seeds 35
Corn on the Cob 55
Eggplant Slices, Grilled 61
Ginger Carrots 50
Green Beans 82

Greens, Steamed 17
Mashed Potatoes 75
Oven Roasted Potatoes 16
Peas with Oregano and Mint 29
Potatoes Provencal 35
Potato Wedges with Rosemary 28
Roast Parsley Potatoes 82
Spiced Beets 83
Sweet Potatoes with Pineapple 76
Zucchini Slices 40

Desserts
Apple Crisp 64
Carob Mint Cookies 92
Chocolate Covered Strawberries 25
Fig Spice Cake 85
Frozen Lemon Yogurt Pie 43
Oatmeal Chocolate Chip Bars 71
Peach Cobbler 51
Pineapple Upsidedown Cake 19
Pumpkin Pie 78
Strawberry Mousse 37
Strawberry Short Cake 31
Whipped Topping 37

New Year Day's Dinner

- **Roast Nuggets**
- **Dressing**
- **Oven Roasted Potatoes**
- **Gravy**
- **Black Eyed Peas**
- **Steamed Greens**
- **Fresh Cranberry Orange Relish**
- **Waldorf Salad**
- **Pineapple Upside Down Cake**

Ah, a New Year, a new beginning. A resolution to exercise more, to eat right, to enjoy the foods I eat. On this feast day, millions of Americans sit down to a huge holiday dinner (usually at half time). After eating the wrong foods, they are more likely to take a nap than a walk. But the new you can do it a smarter way and enjoy healthy versions of traditional dishes. Try old favorites cooked in heart healthy ways and feel good after the feast.

In many parts of this great country, a traditional food to serve on New Year's is Black Eyed Peas. Eating these is said to bring good luck for all the year. So put a bowl of black eyed peas on the table, but also try something new like oven roasted nuggets made of gluten, the protein of wheat. High in protein, low in fat, chewy in texture, gluten or seitan is simple to prepare.

Roasted Gluten Nuggets

These are chewy and good. If you can't obtain the flavored instant gluten, add a teaspoon each of sage, thyme and marjoram to regular vital wheat gluten. before you mix it with the broth.

Mix together well:
   2 cups chicken-flavor instant gluten
   2 cups vegetable broth

Break off small balls and stretch and flatten these into 24 pieces. Drop them into a kettle of boiling water that has **1 Tablespoon of soy sauce added**. Cover and simmer over medium low heat for 45 minutes. Drain. Mix for a coating:

1 cup very fine bread crumbs
1 Tablespoon nutritional yeast
1 teaspoon paprika

Pat the nuggets in the coating. Preheat oven to 350 degrees. Lightly spray a large baking sheet with non-stick spray. Place nuggets on sheet. Bake for 10 minutes, turn over and bake 10 minutes more. Place nuggets on a platter. Garnish with sprigs of parsley and wedges of lemon. Serves 8. *210 calories per serving.*

Dressing

Our dressing is flavorful and low in fat. If bread is not dry, cut into cubes and dry it out in a low oven. Whole wheat sour dough bread is excellent.

6 cups day old bread in half-inch cubes
2 cups diced celery
1 medium onion, chopped small
1 cup broth
2 Tablespoons minced parsley
2 teaspoons sage (rub it in your hands)
1 teaspoon thyme
1/8 teaspoon black pepper

Combine the bread and celery in a large bowl. Simmer the onion in the broth until tender, pour onion and broth over the bread. Stir in the parsley and seasonings. If desired, add **2 cups of sliced mushrooms.** Spray a 2 quart casserole dish with non stick vegetable oil, spoon dressing into dish. Cover lightly with foil and bake at 350 degrees for 40 minutes. If you like a drier dressing uncover the dish the last 10 minutes of cooking. Serves 8. *55 calories in a 1/2 cup serving.*

Oven Roasted Potatoes

Oven roasted potatoes can bake at the same time as the nuggets. Peel **6 medium large potatoes** and cut each in quarters. Parboil for 10 minutes in **3 cups water.** Drain well. Spray a large baking pan with non-stick olive oil spray, put potatoes in the pan in a single layer and spray again. Bake at 350 degrees for 15 minutes, gently turn potatoes over, using a pancake turner. Sprinkle a little paprika on top. Spray the tops, continue to bake another 15 minutes or until lightly browned. Serves 6. *116 calories per serving.*

Gravy

The secret of our good tasting low fat gravy is in a chef's trick of toasting the flour and using flavorful vegetable broth for the liquid.

1/3 cup unbleached flour
2 Tablespoons nutritional yeast
2 tablespoons olive oil
2 1/2 cups vegetable broth
a little black pepper
1 to 2 teaspoons soy sauce

Heat a heavy bottomed 2-quart sauce pan. (A cast iron skillet will also do.) Place the flour in the pan and cook over medium high heat a few minutes, stirring, until you can faintly smell the flour as it begins to slightly change color. Be careful not to scorch it. Remove from heat and add the yeast and oil, stir well and add the broth. Return to heat and use a whisk to blend smoothly as it cooks and thickens. Add pepper and soy sauce to taste. This can be made ahead and reheated just before serving. Keep covered. Makes 2 cups gravy. *A 1/4 cup serving has 30 calories.*

Black Eyed Peas

This small tan colored legume has one black "eye" and a mellow flavor. Soak **2 cups of rinsed black eyes** overnight. Rinse, place with 8 cups water in a 3 quart kettle. Add **2 or 3 cloves of garlic and a bay leaf** to the cooking water. Bring to a boil, reduce heat and simmer until tender, about 50 minutes. Drain, remove bay leaf, season with a little salt and pepper. In the South, black eyed peas are often served with a side dish of salsa. *A 1/2 cup serving has 99 calories.*

Steamed Greens

While the black eyed peas are simmering on top of the stove you can steam some greens of your choice: collards, mustard or turnip greens, kale or fresh spinach. It is helpful in washing greens to use a large pan of slightly warm water with a little salt added. Don't overcrowd the pan. Rinse greens and cook to desired degree of tenderness. Excellent served with a splash of balsamic vinegar, which has a unique woodsy flavor from being aged in casks. *1/2 cup serving has 21 calories.*

Waldorf Salad

This is crisp and crunchy and a traditional salad in many homes. Be sure to use high quality apples.

3 Granny Smith apples, diced, seeds removed
1 cup celery, diced
1/4 cup raisins (optional)
Juice of 1 lemon
1/4 cup lo-cal eggless mayonnaise
1/4 cup nonfat soy yogurt
1/2 teaspoon celery seed
dash of celery salt if desired

Combine apples, celery and raisins. Mix the lemon juice with mayonnaise and yogurt. Combine all ingredients and mix well. Arrange a lettuce leaf on each salad plate and top with a scoop of the salad. Makes 8 servings. *112 calories per half cup serving.*

Fresh Cranberry Orange Relish

This can be made quickly in a food processor and is a marvelous accompaniment to the holiday feast. Make it the day before so flavors mingle.

2 cups fresh cranberries
1 medium orange, cut up, seeds removed
1 medium red apple, cored, cut up
1/4 to 1/3 cup sweetener of choice

Wash and drain the cranberries, removing any withered berries. Place in the food processor with the cutting blade, adding the cut up orange, apple and sweetener. Whiz until pieces are coarsely chopped, being careful not to puree. Taste to adjust sweetness, it should be tart but not bitter. Place in a covered jar and chill several hours or overnight. *One tablespoon has 22 calories.*

Pineapple Upside Down Cake

This is usually made with canned pineapple slices but a fresh pineapple may be used. Many supermarkets now offer fresh ones already cored and peeled.

Lightly oil the bottom and sides of a 6 x 10 inch pan. Combine in a saucepan:

1/4 cup brown sugar
1/3 cup juice from pineapple
1 Tablespoon safflower oil

Bring to a boil, stirring. Remove from heat, pour into baking dish. Slice the fresh pineapple into 8 slices about a half inch thick. Cut slices in half and arrange in two rows on bottom of pan. Stir together for the batter:

3/4 cup white sugar
1 1/2 cups unbleached flour
2 teaspoons baking powder
1/4 teaspoon salt
1/4 teaspoon nutmeg
2/3 cup soy milk
2 Tablespoons safflower oil
2 teaspoons vanilla

Spoon batter evenly over pineapple. Preheat oven to 350 degrees and bake cake 30 to 35 minutes. Cool in pan a few minutes. Run a knife around the edge. Place platter over pan and invert cake, spooning out sauce left in pan. Cool, cut in 8 squares. *220 calories per serving.*

Valentine's Day Romantic Supper

- Spicy Boullion Warmer

- Angel's Hair Pasta Primavera

- Fresh Asparagus with Lemon Butter

- Tomato Aspic Salad

- Chocolate Covered Strawberries

Valentine's Day

Whether you plan a romantic dinner for two or a luncheon or supper party for several close friends, red is the color to use in place mats and napkins. The decorations are hearts and flowers. Get out your best china and crystal so that the table sparkles.

The menu features red, with cherry tomatoes in the pasta and the aspic salad. Our dessert is very special on this occasion: Chocolate Covered Strawberries. If you don't entertain on the 14th of February, you can celebrate the holiday by making a plate of these very elegant treats to give to someone you love.

This same menu could be used to celebrate Washington's Birthday or President's Day as red is the theme color for those holidays.

Be My Valentine

Spicy Boullion Warmer

Heat **4 cups vegetable broth**, add **1 Tablespoon vegetarian Worchestershire** sauce and a few drops of **hot pepper sauce**. Pour into bowls and garnish each with a twisted thin slice of **lemon**. Serve as a first course. There are only about *20 calories in a 2/3 cup serving*.

Angel's Hair Pasta Primavera

Colorful with the bright red of cherry tomatoes and the emerald green of broccoli, this is a delicious entree for special guests.

12 ounces angel's hair pasta
2 cups broccoli flowerets
4 teaspoons olive oil
1 medium onion, chopped
1 medium green pepper, diced
2 cloves garlic, sliced
8 ounces mushrooms, sliced
16 cherry tomatoes, cut in half
Soy Parmesan cheese (optional)

Cook the pasta in boiling water for 3 or 4 minutes until just tender. Drain and keep warm. Heat a kettle of water, drop in the broccoli flowerets and cook 2 minutes only. Drain and set aside. Heat a large skillet and put in half the olive oil, tilting the pan so the oil covers the bottom. Add the onion and green pepper cook over medium high heat for a few minutes, add the garlic and cook 1 minute more. Remove vegetables to a warm dish. Add the remaining oil to the hot pan, add the sliced mushrooms. Cook just a few minutes, until the mushrooms begin to give out juice, then put the broccoli flowerets into the skillet and cook a minute. Add the peppers and onions. Stir together and add the halves of cherry tomatoes, stir just a minute then toss with the cooked pasta. Arrange on a big round platter, garnishing with a few sprigs of parsley. Sprinkle with a little soy parmesan cheese if desired. This will serve 6 generously. *280 calories per serving.*

Fresh Asparagus with Lemon

Snap off the woody stems from **1 pound of fresh asparagus,** rinse stalks to remove any sand and cut on the diagonal in 2 inch lengths. Have a kettle of boiling water ready, drop in the stems first and cook for 5 minutes, then drop in the tips and cook 5 or 6 minutes more. Drain and place in a warm serving bowl with **2 teaspoons of olive oil.** Sprinkle with **juice of half a lemon** and a **dash of black pepper.** *32 calories in a 1/2 cup serving.*

Tomato Aspic Salad

Using kanten flakes, also called agar, makes an old recipe new. Make the day before so it has plenty of time to become firm.

3 Tablespoons kanten flakes
3 cups tomato juice
1 small onion, cut up
3 sprigs of parsley
1 Tablespoon cider vinegar
4 whole cloves
1 teaspoon sugar

Combine all ingredients except kanten flakes in a 2 quart saucepan. Bring to a boil, reduce heat and simmer 10 minutes. Strain the juice, add the kanten and cook over medium heat 5 minutes so kanten is completely dissolved. Stir in:

1 cup chopped celery

Spray a serving dish with nonstick vegetable oil. Pour salad in and chill until firm. To serve, arrange romaine leaves on each plate and spoon the aspic onto the greens. Serves 8. *20 calories per serving.*

Chocolate Covered Strawberries

In sophisticated cities these delicious treats are sold in fancy boxes at very fancy prices. You will find them simple to make at home.

24 large fresh strawberries, with leaves

Line a platter with waxed paper. Wash berries gently but do not remove the green leaves. Dry them gently on paper towels. Melt in a small pan set in a pan of hot water over low heat:

6 ounces carob or chocolate chips

You may need to reheat the chocolate as you work. Do not try to melt the chocolate over direct heat. Carefully hold each berry by its green leaves and dip it into the melted chocolate to cover the bottom half of the berry, leaving some red showing. Place each on the paper to firm. Chill until ready to serve. *42 calories per berry.*

The Easter Feast

- Tofu with Shiitake Mushrooms
- Potato Wedges with Rosemary
- Peas with Oregano and Mint
- Chilled Three Bean Salad
- Strawberry Shortcake

EASTER DINNER

The days of the big Easter parade may be gone, but dying or painting colorful Easter eggs is still a custom. An interesting centerpiece for your dinner table would be decorated eggs tucked into a stand of green grass in an oblong ceramic container. About six weeks before Easter purchase alfalfa seeds from a farm store or co-op and plant them in water in the container. Green grass will actually grow and be about four inches high in time for the holiday.

Our entree is baked slices of tofu with a hearty sauce of fresh shiitake mushrooms. The baked potato wedges are a treat your family will want again, easier to make than French fries and much healthier. For dessert, an old fashioned strawberry shortcake is sure to please.

Tofu with Shiitake Mushrooms

The seasoned tofu is baked as the smoky flavored sauce simmers on the stove.

Wrap in a towel and set aside for 10 minutes before slicing:
> 16 oz. firm tofu

Mix on a plate for the coating:
> 1/2 cup flour
> 2 Tablespoons nutritional yeast
> 1 teaspoon paprika
> 1/2 teaspoon salt
> 1/4 teaspoon black pepper

Preheat oven to 350 degrees. Spray a baking sheet with olive oil. Slice tofu into 12 to 14 pieces and dip each into the coating. Arrange on baking sheet. Bake for 10 minutes, turn slices over and bake 10 minutes more. Serve with Mushroom Sauce. *80 calories per slice.*

Shiitake Mushroom Sauce

Wipe clean, remove stems and slice:
> 4 ounces fresh shiitake mushrooms

Heat a skillet and saute over medium high heat:
> 1 Tablespoon olive oil
> 1 medium onion, chopped fine
> 1/2 teaspoon salt

After 5 minutes, add the mushroom slices (use stems in stock pot) and saute 5 minutes more. Reduce heat to low and add:
> 2 cups vegetable broth
> 1 Tablespoon soy sauce
> 1/2 teaspoon ground ginger
> 1/2 teaspoon ground savory

Cover pan and simmer 15 minutes. Thicken sauce by stirring in a mixture of:

1 Tablespoon cornstarch
1/4 cup cold water

Stir sauce until thick and bubbly. *41 calories per 1/4 cup.*

Potato Wedges with Rosemary

A delicious way to prepare a healthy vegetable. Use fresh rosemary if you have it.

6 fairly large potatoes
2 Tablespoons olive oil
2 teaspoons dried rosemary
2 Tablespoons freshly minced parsley

Peel the potatoes and cut into thick lengthwise wedges. Drop into a kettle of boiling water and cook 10 minutes, drain. Place the oil in a large bowl. Put partially cooked potatoes into the bowl and stir gently until all are evenly coated with oil. Spray a large baking sheet with non-stick oil. Arrange potatoes on the tray in a single layer. Sprinkle the potatoes with rosemary. Preheat oven to 350 degrees and bake potatoes about 30 minutes, test with a fork for doneness. Potatoes should be golden brown and tender. Remove from baking sheet with a pancake turner so they do not break. Sprinkle potatoes with parsley and add a dash of salt if desired. Serve hot. Serves 8. *110 calories per serving.*

Peas with Oregano and Mint

Enjoy the flavors of this herb seasoned vegetable.
> 16 oz. package frozen peas
> pinch of salt
> 1 teaspoon dried mint leaves
> 1 teaspoon oregano

Bring a half cup of water to a boil and drop in peas, cover and cook about 5 minutes until peas are tender. Drain. Toss with the pinch of salt, the mint and oregano. Serves 6. *65 calories in 1/2 cup.*

Three Bean Salad

Make several hours ahead or the day before so flavors blend.
> 2 cups (16 oz. can) French cut green beans
> 2 cups (16 oz. can) red kidney beans
> 2 cups (16 oz. can) garbanzo or ceci beans
> 1/3 cup apple cider vinegar
> 1/4 cup sugar
> 1/2 teaspoon salt
> 1/2 cup diced celery
> 1/2 cup diced green pepper
> 1/2 cup diced red onion

Drain the beans and place in a glass salad bowl. Bring to a boil in a small saucepan the vinegar, sugar and salt. Pour over the beans and toss to mix well. Cover and let stand several hours. Just before serving stir in the celery, pepper and onion, add a dash of **black pepper.** Serves 8. *145 calories per half cup serving.*

Strawberry Shortcake

This is a fitting finale for a feast. The shortcake is a rich biscuit dough, baked in one pan but so it will separate into two layers. Frozen berries can be thawed for use if fresh are not available.

Rinse, remove the hulls and cut in half:
1 quart strawberries

Sprinkle with:
2 Tablespoons sugar

Heat oven to 375 degrees. Lightly oil bottom and sides of an 8-inch round cake pan. Stir together:
2 cups flour
2 Tablespoons sugar
2 teaspoons baking powder
1/2 teaspoon salt

Combine and add to dry ingredients:
1/4 cup safflower oil
3/4 cup vanilla soymilk

Knead the dough together and divide into two balls, patting each out into an 8-inch circle. Place one piece of dough in pan, spray the top lightly with oil, place other circle on top. Bake for 25 minutes until lightly golden in color. Remove, cool for 5 minutes, tip out on platter and slice cake into two rounds. Spoon half the berries on the bottom round, top with the other half and spoon remaining berries over. Cut into 8 wedges to serve. If desired, top with low fat frozen vanilla yogurt. It is also good with tofu whipped topping. *122 calories per serving without any topping.*

Celebrate Mother's Day

- Medallions with Plums

- Scalloped Potatoes Provencal

- Broccoli with Sesame Seeds

- Melon Ring Salad with Yogurt

- Strawberry Mousse

Mother's Day

England gave recognition to mothers by observing a day called "Mothering Sunday" as far back as the 18th century. Julia Ward Howe suggested in 1872 that the United States celebrate Mother's Day but the idea did not gain wide acceptance. In 1907, Anna Jarvis began actively campaigning for nationwide observance and in 1915 President Woodrow Wilson was authorized by Congress to proclaim annual national observance of Mother's Day on the second Sunday in May of each year.

It's traditional that a family comes together to honor Mother on her day. Spring flowers can be picked for a bouquet on the table. The menu should be planned to provide a variety of flavors, colors and aromas but to not make too much work for Mom.

Medallions with Plums

Delicious cutlets made from instant gluten in a rosy sauce with purple plums is an elegant entree.

1 1/2 cups vital wheat gluten
1 1/4 cups water
1 teaspoon thyme
1 teaspoon marjoram
1 Tablespoon soy sauce

Mix wet and dry ingredients, shape into a log, place in kettle with 2 quarts water and simmer 45 minutes. Remove gluten and slice into medallions. Make a sauce by draining **one 16 ounce can of purple plums**, add water to juice to make 2 cups liquid. Add **1 Tablespoon cornstarch, 1 teaspoon Dijon mustard, and 1 teaspoon sugar.** Cook over high heat, stirring constantly, until thick and bubbly. Pour over the medallions and top with plums. Serves 6. *188 calories per serving.*

Scalloped Potatoes Provencal

This medley of vegetables is full of flavor and one I make often.

2 pounds russet potatoes, peeled and sliced
1 medium onion, thinly sliced
8 ounces fresh mushrooms, sliced
16 oz. can stewed tomatoes
1 cup broth
2 teaspoons fruity olive oil
Salt and Pepper
1 teaspoon basil

Spray a 3-quart casserole with non-stick vegetable oil. Arrange a layer of potatoes, a layer of onion, repeat, then a layer of half the mushrooms. Dot the top of the vegetables with half the tomatoes and sprinkle with salt and pepper. Repeat these layers. Pour remaining tomatoes, oil and the broth over the top and sprinkle with the basil. Cover the casserole and bake at 350 degrees for 50 to 60 minutes. Remove cover and test with a fork to make certain potatoes are tender. Serves 8. *145 calories per serving.*

Broccoli with Sesame Seeds

Broccoli is considered to be an anti-cancer vegetable and cooked this way it is jade green and delicious.

   1 pound broccoli
   2 teaspoons sesame seeds
   2 cloves garlic, thinly sliced
   2 teaspoons olive oil
   1 Tablespoon soy sauce

Cut the flowers from the broccoli, with about 4 inches of stem on each. Toast the sesame seeds for 3 or 4 minutes over medium high heat in a dry skillet, stirring so they do not scorch. Set seeds aside. Blanch broccoli in a kettle of boiling water, cooking for 2 minutes only. Drain and keep warm. Broccoli should be crisp-tender, not soft. Just before serving, heat a large skillet, add the olive oil and when it sizzles drop in the broccoli and garlic slices and stir fry a few minutes, just until the broccoli is hot. Pour the soy sauce over the broccoli and spoon it into a warm dish. Sprinkle the toasted sesame seeds on top. This can be served at room temperature. 6 servings. *48 calories each serving.*

Melon Rings with Yogurt

Canteloupe combines great flavor with good nutrition. It is very high in Vitamin A and in potassium.

1 medium large canteloupe
12 lettuce leaves
6 oz. blueberry yogurt

Slice the melon into 6 slices. Remove the outer rind and the seeds from each slice. Arrange lettuce on each salad plate and place a melon ring on the lettuce. Place a spoonful of yogurt in the center of each ring. If desired, top with a few fresh berries. Serve chilled. 8 servings. *72 calories each serving.*

Strawberry Mousse

This tempting dessert combines berries and tofu.
20 oz. pkg. frozen strawberries,
unsweetened, sliced
1/4 cup sugar
3 Tablespoons kanten flakes
1 cup juice from berries

Mix berries and sugar, let stand 30 minutes. Drain, saving juice. If you do not have one cup of juice add water. Cook kanten and juice 5 minutes, cool. Fold berries into kanten, chill. Fold in the tofu whipped topping, recipe below. Pour into parfait glasses and chill. Serves 6. *145 calories..*

Whipped Topping

Blend thoroughly in a food processor or blender:
10.5 oz. package silken tofu
1/3 cup confectioners sugar
1/4 cup safflower oil
1 teaspoon vanilla
pinch of salt

Blend until smooth. Keep chilled.

Memorial Day Luncheon

- Indonesian Style Tofu

- Grilled Zucchini Slices

- Marinated Vegetable Salad

- Mexican Rice Casserole

- Lemon Pie with Gingersnap Crust

MEMORIAL DAY

We proudly celebrate this patriotic holiday with flags waving, bands playing and everyone marching in the big parade. In many parts of the country this is the day that officially ushers in summer and dining out of doors. So, invite a friend to join you for a meal on the patio after the parade,

Our menu for Memorial Day features tofu, which is high in protein, low in fat and has no cholesterol. Marinated and baked in this Indonesian peanut sauce, it is delicious. Other delectable dishes that round out the menu can be made the day before: the vegetable salad, a rice casserole and the frozen dessert.

Indonesian Style Tofu

Combine in blender:
- 1 Tablespoon minced raw ginger
- 1 clove garlic, minced
- 2 Tablespoons soy sauce
- 2 Tablespoons peanut butter
- 1/4 cup boiling water
- 1 Tablespoon lemon juice
- 1 Tablespoon brown sugar
- 1/2 teaspoon ground coriander
- 1/2 teaspoon cumin
- 1/4 teaspoon cayenne

Wrap **16 oz. firm tofu** in a towel, pat dry, slice into 12 pieces. Spray a 7x10" pan, arrange the tofu slices and pour the sauce on them. Marinate for an hour or more. Preheat oven to 375 degrees, bake tofu 25 minutes. Serves 6. *140 calories per serving.*

Grilled Zucchini Slices

Select firm young squash, 6 to 8 ounces each. Yellow squash can also be used., or some of both.
- 3 small zucchini (7 oz. each)
- 2 Tablespoons soy sauce
- 1 teaspoon dark sesame oil
- 1 teaspoon powdered ginger
- 1/2 teaspoon garlic powder

Wash zucchini but do not peel. Cut in half length-wise and place in shallow baking dish. Mix soy sauce, oil and spices, pour over squash. Let stand for an hour, turning to coat evenly. Spray a non stick skillet, lay slices in pan and cook 4 to 6 minutes on each side. Squash should be tender but not mushy. *18 calories a slice.*

Marinated Vegetable Salad

Make this colorful and flavorful salad ahead, stirring once or twice. Serve in a large glass bowl.

1 bunch broccoli, cut into flowerets
1 head cauliflower, broken into flowerets
1 medium red onion, diced
1/2 cup celery, chopped
1 large carrot, grated

Heat a large kettle of water and drop broccoli and cauliflower pieces into the boiling water and boil for 2 minutes to blanch. Drain, rinse and cool in a pan of ice water. Drain well. Combine all vegetables in a big bowl and toss with a dressing made by mixing:

1/4 cup nonfat soy yogurt
1/4 cup eggless mayonnaise
1 Tablespoon Dijon mustard
2 Tablespoons lemon juice
Dash of garlic powder and black pepper

Cover salad and let stand to blend the flavors. Stir. *9 servings. 54 calories per cup.*

Mexican Rice Casserole

A savory dish that provides protein as well as complex carbohydrates, it can be made ahead and reheated.

1 1/2 cups brown rice
3 1/2 cups vegetable broth
2 teaspoons olive oil
1 medium onion, chopped
1 green pepper, chopped
2 Tablespoons tomato paste
1 teaspoon chili powder
1 teaspoon cumin
1/2 teaspoon garlic powder

Cook rice and broth together until rice is tender and liquid is absorbed, about 50 minutes. Heat a skillet, add oil and tilt pan so oil covers bottom. Add the onion and pepper and stir fry until soft. Add spices and tomato paste. Mix into the cooked rice. Add a little broth if rice appears dry. Cover, keep cold. The next day, bring to room temperature and bake 30 minutes in a hot oven. This will serve 8. *150 calories per serving.*

Lemon Pie with Gingersnap Crust

A delectable dessert with chocolate curls on top comple-menting the lemon filling and the gingery crust. This can be made the day before the party. Frozen raspberry yogurt is also delicious.

Gingersnaps can be placed in a plastic bag and carefully crushed into fine crumbs. Mix and spread evenly on the bottom of a 9 inch pie pan:

14 gingersnaps, crushed into crumbs
1 Tablespoon safflower oil
2 Tablespoons apple juice

Preheat oven to 350 degrees and bake crust 10 minutes. Cool for an hour or more.

Soften enough to spoon into the pie shell and spread evenly:

1 quart low-fat frozen lemon yogurt

Use a vegetable peeler to shave a plain **chocolate bar** into thin curls over the top of the pie. Cover pie and freeze until ready to serve. Cut pie into 8 wedges to serve, use a pancake turner to lift slices onto plates. *225 calories per serving.*

Celebrate Father's Day

- Baked Lasagne

- Greek Salad

- Ginger Carrots

- Fresh Peach Cobbler

Father's Day

Efforts to have a day of recognition for Fathers were underway as far back as 1910, but it wasn't until 1972 that the third Sunday in June officially became a national observance of Father's Day. The holiday is celebrated in Canada as well as many other countries.

It's appropriate that on the day we express our appreciation of Dad we plan a meal featuring his favorite foods and prepare them in a be-kind-to-the-arteries style that has little fat and no cholesterol. We've used crumbled tofu in the big pasta dish to reduce calories. The Greek salad is unusually good and the ginger carrots add zest to the menu. The first peaches of summer can be made into a yummy cobbler. Dad can sit back and relax while the rest of the family prepares a feast for him.

Lasagne

This flavorful recipe makes a large pan that can serve 12. Any extra portions can be frozen for later enjoyment.

Spray a large oblong baking dish with nonstick vegetable oil spray. Cook **16 ounces of lasagne curly edged noodles** according to the package directions, adding them to the boiling water one at a time and pushing with a wooden spoon so they do not stick together. Stir occasionally so they stay separate. When noodles are tender, drain, then cover with cold water while preparing layers, taking out a few at a time to dry. Have a soft towel ready to dry noodles.

For the sauce, whiz in the blender:
> **1 large (30 oz.) can plum tomatoes**

Combine in a kettle with:
> **1 (6 oz.) can tomato paste**
> **2 (6 oz.) cans water**
> **2 teaspoons oregano**
> **1 teaspoon basil**
> **1/2 teaspoon garlic powder**
> **2 Tablespoons minced fresh parsley**
> **1 teaspoon sugar**

Bring the sauce to a simmer and cook about 15 minutes.

Have ready:
8 ounces mushrooms, sliced
2 small zucchini (1 pound), thinly sliced
1 (16 oz.) package firm tofu
2 Tablespoons soy parmesan cheese

Add the mushrooms to the tomato sauce. Pour a little sauce on the bottom of the baking pan, tilting pan to cover evenly. Remove 4 or 5 noodles from the water for each layer, drying on a soft towel. Put one layer of noodles in the pan, overlapping each slightly. Spread a thin layer of sauce on the noodles. Arrange a layer of the zucchini slices, then another layer of noodles and more sauce. Put spoonfuls of the crumbled tofu on top, spacing evenly. Top with another layer of noodles and the remaining sauce. Sprinkle the parmesan cheese over the top and cover loosely with foil. Place pan on a cookie sheet to catch any drips. Preheat oven to 350°, bake lasagne about 30 minutes, remove the foil. Continue to bake for 30 minutes more. Remove from oven and let stand for 10 minutes before cutting *12 servings at 185 calories each.*

Greek Salad

This is a big colorful salad. The vegetables can be prepared ahead and kept chilled in a plastic bag. The pieces of pita breads are a surprise ingredient but can be prepared ahead and kept in a separate bag. Toss all together with the dressing just before serving.

1 head romaine lettuce
1 medium head iceberg lettuce
1 small red onion, diced
1 large cucumber, sliced
1 green pepper, diced
2 medium tomatoes, cut into 8 wedges each
10 radishes, sliced
2 pita breads

Wash, pat dry and tear up the romaine and iceberg lettuce leaves. Slice and dice the other vegetables. Toast the pita breads, separate each into 2 pieces and cut into 1 inch size pieces. Keep pita separate from the vegetables and add at the last minute so they remain crisp.

For the **dressing**, shake up in a little jar and set aside:

    2 Tablespoons red wine vinegar
    1 Tablespoon water
    1/2 teaspoon dry mustard
    1/2 teaspoon salt
    1 teaspoon basil
    1 teaspoon oregano
    1/8 teaspoon black pepper
    1/4 cup olive oil

Before serving, cut a **garlic clove** in half and rub the sides of a big wooden bowl with the garlic pieces. Toss together in the bowl the vegetables and the dressing. When well mixed, add the pita pieces and toss gently. Serve at once. *12 large servings at 90 calories each.*

Ginger Carrots

Fixed this way, good-for-you carrots take on a whole new dimension. I used to love cooked carrots served with a lot of butter or in a fattening cream sauce. Now I've found this low calorie way of fixing them, and make the dish the day before so the carrots absorb more of the tangy sauce. If the packages of whole baby carrots are not available in your market, you can cut full size peeled carrots into half inch chunks.

1 pound baby carrots
1 quart boiling water

Drop carrots into boiling water and cook 8 to 10 minutes until tender but still firm and not mushy. Prepare the sauce by combining in a quart saucepan:

1/4 cup white wine vinegar
2 Tablespoons frozen apple juice concentrate
1 Tablespoon soy sauce
2 teaspoons minced raw gingerroot

Bring the sauce to a boil, remove from heat. Drain carrots and add to sauce. Stir and let stand an hour or more. Stir occasionally. Just before serving, return pan to heat and warm up. *40 calories per 1/2 cup serving.*

Fresh Peach Cobbler

This is a no-cholesterol version of a favorite dessert, adapted from an old family recipe. Be sure to use sweet, ripe peaches. It is delicious served either warm or cold.

6 to 7 large ripe peaches
2 Tablespoons of sugar
1 Tablespoon of soy margarine

Prepare a 9" x 9" baking dish by spraying with nonstick vegetable spray.

Peel and slice the peaches into the dish. Sprinkle them with sugar and dot with margarine. Preheat the oven to 350 degrees and prepare the batter as follows.

2 teaspoons egg replacer to equal 2 eggs,
dissolved in 1/2 cup of water
1/2 cup sugar
1 cup flour
1 teaspoon baking powder
1 teaspoon vanilla
1/4 teaspoon nutmeg

Beat together the egg product and water. Measure the dry ingredients. Stir together the dry and wet ingredients and pour the batter over the peaches. Bake in a preheated 350 degree oven about 30 minutes until lightly golden. Cut into 9 squares to serve. *225 calories per serving.*

Fourth of July Barbecue

- Relish Tray of Celery and Carrot Sticks
- Barbecued Gluten Ribs
- Grilled Corn on the Cob
- Potato Salad
- Baked Beans
- Sliced Tomatoes with Basil
- Ice Cold Watermelon

The Fourth of July

Bands will be playing and flags will be waving as we celebrate our country's birth of freedom with the big parade. Afterwards you can entertain family and friends at the traditional barbecue. This year the meal will be healthier, with chewy, low calorie gluten ribs to enjoy.

While the savory aroma of grilling ribs fills the air, pass a tray of raw vegetables with a delicious dip or two (see the recipes for New Year's Eve) so people can munch on something without destroying their appetites or diets. Serve frosty glasses of iced tea with lemon slices to quench their thirst.

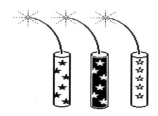

Barbecued Gluten Ribs

The secret of these flavorful ribs is the baking, as they puff up and crisp. They only need reheating on the grill

Mix together:
2 cups instant gluten flour
2 Tablespoons nutritional yeast

Stir in all at once:
1 2/3 cup water
1/3 cup ketchup

Gluten should be quite wet. Roll and stretch into a flat oblong and cut into 24 strips about half inch wide and 6 inches long. Place on lightly oiled baking sheets. Preheat oven to 375 degrees. Bake 15 minutes, strips will puff up.

Turn strips over, prick each with a fork in several places and pour barbecue sauce on ribs. Bake 15 minutes more.

Barbecue Sauce

Combine in a small saucepan:
1/2 cup ketchup
1 Tablespoon brown sugar
1 Tablespoon cider vinegar
1 teaspoon Worcestershire sauce
1/2 teaspoon dry mustard
dash of cayenne

Simmer the sauce about 5 minutes. Taste and add hot red pepper sauce if you like it hotter. This will keep for a week or two in the refrigerator. *26 calories per tablespoon.*

Grilled Corn on the Cob

One of the joys of summer is corn on the cob that goes directly from the field to a refrigerator to keep it sweet and tender. This year, instead of slathering the corn with butter, try this technique for fewer calories.
10 medium ears of corn
2 Tablespoons olive oil
1 Tablespoon soy sauce
2 teaspoons dark corn syrup
2 teaspoons Dijon mustard

Combine in a small saucepan the oil and syrup. Cook a minute to melt. Stir in the soy sauce and mustard and remove from heat. Pull back the husks on the corn but do not remove them. Remove all the corn silk. Use a brush to paint the ears with the sauce, then pull the husks back up, twisting at the end to close each. Place ears on the grill and cook about 20 minutes, rotating several times. Corn can also be done in a microwave oven, allow 14 minutes for 6 ears on high power. Serve hot. *About 100 calories per ear.*

Potato Salad

A holiday meal in summer would not be complete without potato salad, but enjoy a new healthier recipe this year.

3 pounds russet potatoes, well scrubbed
water to cover for boiling
1/3 cup vegetable broth
2 Tablespoons white wine vinegar
1 cup diced celery
1/2 cup chopped green onions
1/4 cup minced fresh parsley

Cook potatoes in their jackets in water to cover until tender. Slip skins off while potatoes are warm and cut potatoes into bite size chunks. Mix the vegetable broth and vinegar and toss with the potatoes. Set aside to cool. Combine for a dressing:

1/3 cup low fat soy yogurt
1/3 cup eggless mayonnaise
1 Tablespoon unsweetened apple juice concentrate
1 teaspoon Dijon-style mustard
dash of salt and pepper

When potatoes are cold, stir in the celery, onions, and parsley and mix potatoes with the dressing. Taste and add a little more mustard or salt if desired. Toss well and chill for at least an hour to blend the flavors. This makes about 8 cups. *100 calories per cup.*

Baked Beans

This is not Aunt Sophie's recipe, but it is a delicious and less fattening version of a classic dish.

    1 large onion chopped
    1/4 cup vegetable broth
    4 cups (two 16 oz. cans) pinto beans
    1 Tablespoon molasses
    1 Tablespoon white vinegar
    1 teaspoon curry powder

Simmer the onion in broth about 10 minutes until it is tender. Preheat oven to 350 degrees. Mix all ingredients, stir well. Put in a heavy casserole dish, and bake for 20 minutes; uncover and bake 40 minutes more. This will make 8 to 10 servings. *146 calories per half cup serving.*

Sliced Tomatoes with Basil

Nothing tastes better than garden fresh tomatoes. Slice 6 or 8 onto a pretty platter. Chop about **1/4 cup of fresh basil** leaves and sprinkle over the tomatoes. Sprinkle with **2 Tablespoons balsamic vinegar**. If you cannot obtain fresh basil, use 2 teaspoons of dried basil. Cover with plastic wrap until time to serve. *About 10 calories a slice.*

Watermelon has 50 calories in a cup.

Labor Day Cook Out

- Pepper Tofu Kebabs

- Eggplant Teriyaki

- Rice Pilaf with Mushrooms

- Coleslaw

- Cucumber Dill Salad

- Apple Crisp

Labor Day

Celebrate the end of summer with one last cook-out and a menu planned to please everyone's health conscious life style. You could grill low fat tofu hot dogs or be creative and try these elegant and colorful Kebabs. They are low in calories and simple to make. Cubes of tofu are marinated in a zesty sauce and then threaded on skewers, alternating with slices of red and green peppers plus little pearl onions. They have a tantalizing aroma and marvelous taste.

Over the same hot coals, grill slices of eggplant that have been marinated in a teriyaki sauce. Slices of green and yellow squash will also work well on the grill. If it should rain, and the party moves indoors, these foods can be broiled in your oven. Serve a hot Rice Pilaf with Mushrooms as an accompaniment and a less fattening version of traditional Coleslaw. Top this splendid meal with a fresh Apple Crisp warm from the oven and you'll sigh with satisfaction over an enjoyable feast that did not destroy your diet.

Pepper and Tofu Kebabs

Wrap **16 ounces firm tofu** in a towel and set aside while making marinade. Combine in a medium size bowl:

> Juice of 1 lemon
> 2 Tablespoons olive oil
> 2 cloves thinly sliced garlic
> 1 teaspoon oregano
> 1 teaspoon marjoram
> 1 teaspoon cumin
> 1 teaspoon paprika
> 1/8 teaspoon cayenne

Cut tofu into one inch cubes and add to the marinade, toss to coat, cover and chill an hour or more, turn occasionally to coat evenly. If you plan to use wooden skewers, soak them in cold water 30 minutes so the ends do not burn. Prepare the vegetables:

> 2 large green peppers, cut into 1 inch squares
> 2 sweet red peppers, cut into 1 inch squares
> 24 pearl onions (from a 15 oz. jar)

On each skewer thread tofu cubes, placing slices of red and green peppers before and after each tofu cube plus the little white onions. Keep skewers in marinade until cooking time. When the coals are ready, place kebabs on grill and cook about 10 minutes on each side, turning and basting with leftover marinade. This makes 8 kebabs. *122 calories per kebab.*

Eggplant Teriyaki

Buy a fairly large, firm **eggplant**, about 1 1/2 pounds. Wash and slice crosswise into half-inch slices. Sprinkle slices with salt as you place them in a large bowl. Let stand 30 minutes then rinse slices off. This process makes eggplant more mellow. Place the slices in marinade to soak.

> **Teriyaki Marinade:**
> 1/2 cup low sodium soy sauce
> 1 Tablespoon vinegar
> 2 teaspoons fresh chopped gingerroot
> 1 clove garlic, sliced thinly
> 1 teaspoon molasses

Let stand an hour or more, turning once or twice. Grill slices about 7 to 10 minutes on each side until lightly browned, basting with the sauce when turning. *Only 30 calories per slice.*

Grilled Green or Yellow Squash

Choose several small squash that weigh not more than a half pound each. Wash them and cut in half lengthwise. Brush with the teriyaki marinade and grill until golden brown, brushing again when each is turned. Cook until tender but still firm. *28 calories per slice.*

Rice Pilaf with Mushrooms

An aromatic and satisfying casserole that supplies complex carbohydrates.

2 cups brown rice
4 1/2 cups water
12 ounces mushrooms
1 medium onion, chopped
1 Tablespoon olive oil
1 teaspoon dried savory
1 teaspoon dried thyme
1/2 teaspoon garlic powder
1/2 teaspoon salt
dash of black pepper

Cook the rice and water until the rice is tender and the liquid is absorbed, about 50 minutes: Set cooked rice aside. Prepare the mushrooms by rinsing, wiping dry and slicing thinly. Heat a large skillet and add the oil, tilting pan so the bottom is coated. Put in the chopped onion and stir fry about 5 minutes over medium high heat. Add the mushrooms and cook and stir a few minutes until mushrooms begin to brown. Sprinkle mushrooms with the herbs, salt and pepper. Remove pan from heat and combine the onions and mushrooms with the cooked rice, mixing well. Heap the mixture into a pretty baking dish. If made ahead, keep covered. Warm in a moderate oven or microwave until the rice is hot before serving. Makes about 6 cups. *65 calories in a 1/2 cup serving.*

Coleslaw

Here's a reduced calorie version of a classic salad.

Combine in a large glass bowl:
    6 cups finely shredded green cabbage
    1 cup shredded carrot
    4 green onions, thinly sliced with green part
    2 Tablespoons minced fresh parsley

In a small bowl stir together:
    1/2 cup low fat soy yogurt
    2 Tablespoons apple cider vinegar
    1 Tablespoon olive oil
    1 teaspoon sugar
    1/2 teaspoon celery seed
    dash of salt and pepper

Pour the dressing over the vegetables and toss to mix well. Taste to adjust the salt. Cover and chill for at least 2 hours to blend the flavors, stirring once or twice. Toss well just before serving. A nice variation is to add a small can of **crushed unsweetened pineapple** or a cup of **red grapes** cut in half. *52 calories in a 1/2 cup serving.*

Cucumber Dill Salad

This develops flavor when made ahead. You'll like the refreshing taste.

> 2 medium cucumbers, thinly sliced
> 1 small onion, thinly sliced
> 1 teaspoon salt
> 1/4 cup reduced calorie tofu sour cream
> 1/4 cup nonfat soy yogurt
> 1 Tablespoon snipped dill weed

Scrub the cucumbers well, trim ends. Slice the cucumbers and the onion into a medium size bowl, sprinkling with salt as you go. Add some ice cubes to the bowl, cover, let stand 30 minutes. Rinse and drain the vegetables, pressing out any excess liquid. Mix the sour cream, yogurt and dill. Stir in the cucumbers and chill. Serves 8. *36 calories per serving.*

Apple Crisp

Enjoy a hearty helping of this delectable dessert without feelings of guilt. It is delicious served warm or cold.

2 1/2 pounds Granny Smith apples
1 teaspoon cinnamon, divided
1/4 cup water
1/4 cup orange juice
3/4 cup rolled oats
1/2 cup flour
1/4 cup brown sugar, packed
3 Tablespoons safflower oil
1 teaspoon grated orange rind

Spray a 9" x 13" pan with nonstick vegetable oil spray. Peel and core the apples and slice into the pan. Sprinkle apples with 1/2 teaspoon of the cinnamon and pour the water and orange juice over the apples. Preheat the oven to 375 degrees. In a mixing bowl combine the remaining cinnamon, the oatmeal, flour, brown sugar, oil and orange rind. Mix well. Spoon this mixture evenly over the top of the apples. Bake 30 to 35 minutes, use a fork to be sure apples are tender. Remove pan from oven, serve warm or chilled. 8 servings. *168 calories per serving.*

Halloween Party

- Spiced Apple Juice
- Popcorn
- Tortilla Chips
- Mexican Bean Dip
- Pita Pizzas with Mushrooms,
  Peppers and Onions
- Tossed Two Green Salad
- Oatmeal Chocolate Chip Bars

Halloween

This is the night of ghosties and goblins, of trick and treat for the youngsters and a good night for a party of grown ups. Adults like to dress up, too, (why should kids have all the fun?) so suggest guests wear costumes and award a prize for originality. Use black and orange streamers for decorations. A jack o'lantern can serve as the centerpiece on a buffet table. After they eat, guests may want to watch a horror movie or turn the lights down low and take turns telling ghost stories.

Keep the menu simple. Offer appetizers of air-popped pop corn and non-fat tortilla chips with homemade low calorie bean dip. Pita Pizzas are easy to make; peppers, mushrooms and onions are low calorie toppings. Toss a big salad. For dessert, pass delicious bars.

Spiced Apple Juice

This is refreshing and not too sweet.

Cook for 3 minutes in a small saucepan:
1 cup brewed tea
1 teaspoon cinnamon
pinch of cloves

Pour tea over ice cubes in a big pitcher and add:
1 quart unsweetened apple juice, chilled
1/2 quart club soda, chilled

A 6 ounce serving has 20 calories.

Mexican Bean Dip

Avoid any commercial dip that contains lard. It's easy to make your own tasty low fat dip. You can make this with pinto beans or black eyed peas.

Combine in a food processor or blender:
1 (16 oz.) can red kidney beans, drained
1 Tablespoon ketchup
1 teaspoon onion juice
1 teaspoon chili powder
1 teaspoon cumin
1/4 teaspoon garlic powder
few drops hot sauce

Whiz until blended. Taste to determine the amount of hot sauce you wish to add. Add a little liquid from the beans if it is too thick. This is best made ahead so flavors mingle. Serve with low fat tortilla chips. *62 calories in 1/4 cup dip.*

Pita Pizzas

This is a recipe you will use again and again because the individual pizzas are filling and low in calories. Use the whole wheat pita breads and almost-no calorie toppings like mushrooms, peppers and onions.

6 whole wheat pita breads
1 (8 oz.) can tomato sauce
1 teaspoon oregano
1 teaspoon basil
1 cup (4 oz.) sliced mushrooms
1 green pepper, chopped
1 medium onion, chopped
crushed red chili peppers to taste
3 Tablespoons grated soy Parmesan cheese

Mix the tomato sauce with the oregano and basil. Spread it evenly on the pitas. Top each circle with some mushrooms, chopped peppers and onions. Sprinkle a little grated Parmesan on each pizza. Preheat the oven to 400 degrees. Place pizzas in the hot oven, directly on the oven racks. Bake 6 to 8 minutes. Serve hot. *268 calories per pizza.*

Tossed Two Green Salad

In this pretty salad a light green lettuce contrasts with the dark green spinach. Slices of crisp red apple provide an accent.

> 1 head of romaine lettuce, rinsed
> 1/2 pound spinach, washed and patted dry
> 1 red apple
> 1/4 cup diced red onion
> 2 Tablespoons white wine vinegar
> 2 Tablespoons water
> 2 Tablespoons olive oil
> 2 Tablespoons minced parsley
> 1 teaspoon dried dill weed
> Salt and pepper to taste

Remove stems from spinach. Tear up the lettuce and spinach leaves and put into a large salad bowl. Core and slice the apple, add with the onion just before serving. In a small jar, shake up the vinegar, water, oil, parsley and dill. Add salt and pepper to taste. Toss greens, apple slices and dressing just before serving. This makes 8 servings. *45 calories per serving.*

Oatmeal Chocolate Chip Bars

Delectable bars to satisfy a sweet tooth, excellent packed in a lunch box.

Preheat oven to 350 degrees. Spray an 8" x 8" pan with nonstick vegetable oil spray and dust with flour. Combine in a large mixing bowl:

1 cup rolled oats
1/2 cup unbleached flour
1/2 cup brown sugar, packed
1 teaspoon baking powder
1/2 teaspoon salt
1/2 teaspoon cinnamon
1 cup (6 oz.) semi-sweet carob chips
1 teaspoon egg replacer to equal one egg
1 teaspoon vanilla
1/4 cup canola oil
1/4 cup unsweetened apple juice

Mix all the dry ingredients, then stir in the wet ingredients. Mix well and spoon into prepared pan. Bake 20 to 25 minutes, just until edges begin to pull away from the pan. Do not overbake. Bars will be firmer as they cool. Take out of oven and cut into 18 bars, lifting onto a plate while still warm. *103 calories per bar.*

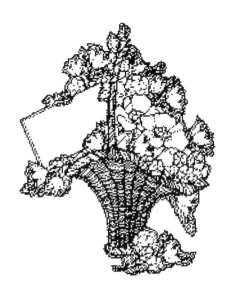

Thanksgiving Dinner

- Roast Gluten
- Cornbread Dressing
- Mashed Potatoes
- Gravy
- Sweet Potatoes with Pineapple
- Baked Onions
- Cranberry Sauce
- Lettuce Salad with Russian Dressing
- Pumpkin Pie

Thanksgiving Day

Once upon a time the pilgrims and Indians feasted together to celebrate a bountiful harvest. Today all across America families come together to say "Thanks" for being alive in a country at peace. Many vegetarians will enjoy Roast Gluten, a healthy alternative to the traditional big bird. It used to take all day to prepare the gluten, separating the protein part of flour from the starch by many rinsings in cold water. Today we can buy instant gluten to mix with broth and simmer or bake.

The other items on our holiday menu are traditional foods, like mashed potatoes, dressing, gravy, and even pumpkin pie. But today these can be prepared in less fattening ways. We no longer cook with quantites of butter and cream, the way that grandmother did, but our food is flavorful and much healthier.

Roast Gluten

Measure into a bowl and stir together:
- 2 cups vital wheat gluten
- 2 Tablespoons nutritional yeast
- 1 teaspoon thyme
- 1 teaspoon marjoram

In a quart measure, combine:
- 2 cups vegetable broth
- 1 Tablespoon soy sauce

Mix wet and dry ingredients together, knead gluten and pack into a large loaf pan.

Slice **1 onion** over the top of the gluten and pour over it:
- 2 cups hot water
- 2 Tablespoons soy sauce

Lay a piece of foil lightly over the top of loaf. Preheat oven to 350 degrees and bake roast about 1 and 1/2 hours. Let cool a little before slicing. Any liquid remaining in the pan is delicious added to the gravy. Serves 8. *103 calories.*

Cornbread Dressing

Dressing can bake while the roast does for a traditional accompaniment.
- 4 cups dry crumbled corn bread
- 2 cups dry cubes whole wheat bread
- 1 medium onion, finely chopped
- 1 cup celery, finely chopped

2 cups vegetable broth
2 Tablespoons minced parsley
1 teaspoon thyme
1 teaspoon sage
1 teaspoon marjoram
1/2 to 1 teaspoon salt
1/4 teaspoon black pepper

Combine the corn bread and dry bread. Simmer the onion and celery in the broth about 10 minutes until tender. Mix onion, broth, parsley and seasonings with bread. Spray a 2-quart baking dish with nonstick vegetable spray, pile dressing in dish. Bake at 350 degrees about 45 minutes. Add a little more broth if it seems too dry. Serves 8. *1/2 cup serving has 110 calories.*

Golden Gravy

This is a gravy that is nutritionally good for you, unlike the fat laden kind we used to know.

Combine in a sauce pan:
2 Tablespoons safflower oil
1/4 cup flour
2 Tablespoons nutritional yeast

Cook these over low heat until bubbling, whisk in:
2 cups vegetable broth
1 teaspoon poultry seasoning
dash of black pepper

Whisk occasionally as it thickens. Let it come to a bubble and simmer over low heat for 1-2 minutes, stirring occasionally. Taste, and add a little salt if needed. Makes 2 cups. *35 calories per 1/4 cup serving.*

Mashed Potatoes

Try this light and fluffy version of an old fashioned comfort food.

6 to 8 medium potatoes
water to cover
1/2 teaspoon salt
1/4 cup soy milk

Peel potatoes and cut each in half. Cover with water and boil until tender, about 20 minutes. Drain and **save** the cooking water. Keep potatoes covered and let stand for 2 minutes in a warm place to dry out. Mash them, adding the salt, milk and about 1/4 cup of the cooking liquid or just enough so potatoes are moist and fluffy. Taste and add a little more salt and pepper if desired. You may wish to stir in

1 to 2 Tablespoons freeze dried chives.

Serve hot. Serves 6 to 8. *120 calories per 1/2 cup.*

Sweet Potatoes with Pineapple

You can make this delicious dish the day before. Forget the calorie loaded marshmallows grandma used, the pineapple adds enough sweetness.

6 medium large sweet potatoes or yams
1 (7 oz.) can crushed pineapple, unsweetened

Line a flat baking pan with foil and set potatoes in the pan. Preheat the oven to 350 degrees. Scrub potatoes and bake them until tender, about 45 minutes. Let cool, remove flesh and discard skins. Spray a shallow baking dish with nonstick vegetable oil. Mash the potatoes until fluffy and pile into the dish. Spoon the pineapple over the potatoes. Cover and refrigerate until ready to bake. Bring to room temperature, then uncover and heat in a 350 to 375 degree oven until hot, about 30 minutes. Serves 6 to 8. *128 calories per serving.*

Baked Onions

A tasty way to include a traditional dish without the heavy cream sauce.

2 (15 oz.) jars of pearl onions
2 Tablespoons salad mustard
2 teaspoons brown sugar
dash of cayenne pepper
4 soda crackers, crushed

Drain and rinse the onions, set aside. Spray a shallow baking dish with non-stick vegetable oil. Heat in a small saucepan the mustard, sugar and cayenne for a few minutes. Mix sauce and the drained onions. Pour into the dish and sprinkle cracker crumbs evenly over the top. Preheat oven to 350 degrees. Bake about 30 minutes. Serves 8. *28 calories per 1/2 cup serving.*

Lettuce Salad with Russian Dressing

Rinse and remove core from **1 large head of iceberg lettuce.** Slice into 8 wedges and place each on a salad plate. Prepare mock Russian Dressing (see page 90). Spoon dressing onto each wedge just before serving. *Less than 20 calories per serving.*

Pumpkin Pie

Here's the traditional dessert but made without eggs to be healthier. It has the usual mellow flavor and smooth texture.

Have an **unbaked 9" pie shell** ready.

Combine in a processor for the filling:
> **10.5 oz. package soft tofu in chunks**
> **3/4 cup brown sugar**
> **3 Tablespoons unbleached flour**
> **16 oz. can of pumpkin**
> **1 teaspoon vanilla**
> **1 teaspoon cinnamon**
> **1/2 teaspoon nutmeg**
> **1/4 teaspoon ginger**

Preheat oven to 375 degrees. Process filling until smooth. Pour into shell. Bake pie for 10 minutes, reduce the heat to 350 degrees. Bake for 45 minutes more. Remove from oven and cool. Cut into 8 slices. *280 calories per slice.* You may wish to top each slice with a spoonful of tofu whipped topping, see recipe on page 37.

Christmas Feast

- Tempeh Sauerbraten
- Roast Parsley Potatoes
- Acorn Squash Rings
- Green Beans
- Spiced Beets
- Spinach Orange Salad
- Fig Spice Cake

Christmas Day

"Over the river and through the woods, to Grandmother's House we go" goes the old refrain as we hang a fragrant wreath on the front door, deck the halls with garlands of holly, open greeting cards and put gaily wrapped presents under the tree. It's a time of year to renew ties with family and friends. The holiday dinner can be substantial without overloading on calories.

Carry out the holiday spirit in red and green, even in the menu. Green appears in the parsley potatoes, green beans and salad, red is in the spicy beets. Our main dish is a savory sauerbraten made with tempeh, a high protein cultured food made from soybeans. `Tis the season to avoid fattening eggnogs. Try spritzers made half and half of fruit juice and seltzer, you will find these are refreshing as well as low in calories. Plan to serve the holiday feast in the middle of the day and keep the other meals of the day light, perhaps hot oatmeal for breakfast and a pot of chili for the evening meal.

Tempeh Sauerbraten

Cut in half crosswise to make two slabs, then cut each into one inch squares:

8 oz. tempeh, defrosted

Combine for the marinade and sauce:

1 cup apple cider
1 cup water
2 Tablespoons ketchup
2 Tablespoons vinegar
1 teaspoon powdered ginger
4 whole cloves, 4 allspice, 4 peppercorns

Let the pieces of tempeh marinate for several hours or even a day or two. Strain, reserving marinade for the sauce. Heat a large skillet and fry tempeh in:

2 Tablespoons oil

When tempeh is brown, remove to a baking dish. Whisk into the reserved marinade:

2 Tablespoons cornstarch

Cook over medium heat until sauce is thick and bubbly, pour over tempeh and serve. Or if made ahead, cover tempeh and sauce and refrigerate. Before serving, bring to room temperature and bake about 20 minutes at 350 degrees. 6 servings. *175 calories.*

Roast Parsley Potatoes

Peel **3 pounds russet potatoes** and cut in quarters. Spray a large baking pan with olive oil spray, arrange potatoes in a single layer. Sprinkle potatoes with **paprika** and **black pepper**. Spray again. Roast at 350 degrees for 45 minutes. Check with a fork for tenderness. Remove to a warm bowl. Sprinkle with **1/4 cup minced fresh parsley.** 8 servings. *116 calories per serving.*

Green Beans

Buy **2 pounds fresh green beans**, trim ends, rinse and slice on the diagonal. Cook in boiling water until tender, 7 to 9 minutes. Drain, sprinkle with **nutmeg** and **black pepper.** Serves 8. *28 calories per 1/2 cup serving.*

Spiced Beets

16 oz. can of sliced beets, drained
1 small onion, sliced thinly
2 Tablespooons vinegar
1/4 cup water
2 Tablespoons sugar
1/2 teaspoon cinnamon
1/4 teaspoon allspice

Combine ingredients in a sauce pan, bring to a boil, add beets and cook about 5 minutes, until beets are heated through. 8 servings. *22 calories in 1/4 cup.*

Acorn Squash Rings

Easy to prepare and an intriguing flavor.
   2 acorn squash, about 12 oz. each
   1 Tablespoon soy sauce
   1 Tablespoon orange marmalade
   1/2 teaspoon powdered ginger

Slice squash crosswise into half-inch slices. Remove seeds and pith. Mix soy sauce, marmalade and ginger. Spray baking sheet with nonstick oil spray. Place rings on pan and brush each slice with the marmalade mixture. Bake at 350 degrees 40 minutes until squash is fork tender. 10 rings. *40 calories each.*

Spinach Orange Salad

Components can be prepared the day before and mixed just before serving.
   7 cups fresh spinach leaves, torn up
   1 large orange, peeled, cut up
   1/2 cup red onion, chopped small

Shake up in a small jar for the dressing:
   2 Tablespoons cold water
   2 Tablespoons red wine vinegar
   2 Tablespoons olive oil
   1/2 teaspoon sugar
   1/2 teaspoon salt

Rinse spinach and pat dry on a towel. Toss together gently the spinach, orange, onion and the dressing just before serving. Serves 8. *45 calories per serving.*

Fig Spice Cake

This is a moist, flavorful cake to enjoy without guilt.

Remove stems from figs, cut up and soak for 1 hour:

> 1 cup cut-up figs
> 1 cup hot water

Measure into a bowl:

> 1/4 cup safflower oil
> 1/3 cup molasses
> 1/3 cup brown sugar, packed
> 1/3 cup water from soaking figs

Preheat oven to 350 degrees and spray a 9"x9" pan. Add to the wet ingredients:

> 1 cup whole wheat flour
> 1 cup unbleached flour
> 2 teaspoons baking powder
> 1/2 teaspoon baking soda
> 1 teaspoon cinnamon
> 1/2 teaspoon nutmeg
> 1/4 teaspoon ground allspice

Stir, adding the figs. Pour into the pan and bake 45 to 50 minutes, until cake begins to pull away from the sides of the pan. Cool. Cut into 9 squares. Dust with a sprinkle of confectioners sugar if desired. *185 calories.*

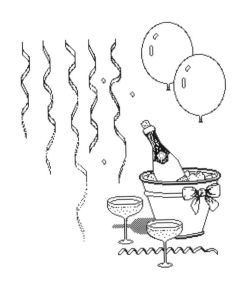

Ring In the New Year

- Holiday Fruit Punch
- Broccoli with Curry Dip
- Cucumber Sticks with Herb Dip
- Celery and Carrot Sticks with
  Russian Dressing
- Apple Slices with Apricot-Ginger Dip
- Pink Party Spread with
  Mini-Bagel Slices
- Sparkly Cherry Tomatoes
- Carob Mint Cookies

New Years Eve

Decorate the room with streamers and balloons. Borrow a big punch bowl and cups for a delicious but low calorie punch. Plan on serving interesting and colorful dips and offer them with "crudities", the fancy French word for raw vegetables.

Set out a bowl or two of pretzels or air-popped popcorn; no one will miss fattening potato chips or salted nuts. It will be a terrific party and everyone can feel good the day after.

Holiday Fruit Punch

Have all ingredients well chilled.

Let steep for 5 minutes:
2 cups boiling water
3 tea bags

Remove bags, add **2 cups water.** Combine with tea in a big punch bowl:
1 quart ice cubes
1 quart pineapple-orange juice, no sugar added
1 quart lemon-lime diet soda

If desired, slice thinly **1 lime** and float slices on the top. Or float scoops of low calorie frozen orange yogurt. *47 calories per 3/4 cup serving.*

Curry Dip

This is best made the day before so flavors can mellow. Curry powders vary in strength so add it a little at a time and take tiny tastes.

Stir together in a small bowl:
>   1/2 cup low fat soy sour cream
>   1/2 cup low calorie eggless mayonnaise
>   2 to 3 teaspoons of curry powder (taste and see)
>   1 teaspoon grated onion juice

Cover and chill the dip until serving time. To serve, arrange broccoli flowerets on a platter around the golden dip. *17 calories per tablespoon.*

Broccoli Flowerets

Rinse and trim stems from:
>   1 large bunch broccoli

With a sharp knife cut off flowers leaving about 3 inches of stem on each. If flowers are too thick, cut in halves or thirds. Bring to a boil 3 quarts water, drop in half the flowerets and boil for 2 minutes only. Have a pan of ice water ready, lift out broccoli pieces with a slotted spoon and drop into the ice water. Into the boiling water put the other half of the broccoli and cook for 2 minutes. Remove first batch from ice water, chill the second. Drain the blanched broccoli, cover and keep cold until time to arrange around the curry dip. *6 calories in 1/4 cup.*

Mixed Herb Dip

If you have fresh herbs available, use two or three times as much as you would use dried herbs. This dip has a fresh tangy taste.

Mix in a small bowl:
> **2/3 cup low fat soy sour cream**
> **1/3 cup low fat eggless mayonnaise**
> **2 Tablespoons minced fresh parsley**
> **2 Tablespoons finely chopped green onions**
> **1 teaspoon each of dried basil, oregano and dill weed**

Cover and chill the dip until serving time. Peel **3 medium cucumbers** and cut into sticks about 3 to 4 inches long and 1/2 inch thick. Keep them in a sealed plastic bag in the refrigerator until ready to arrange on a platter around the dip. You can also use **zucchini;** buy 2 or 3 small zucchini, scrub, trim ends and cut into thin sticks. *26 calories per tablespoon.*

Mock Russian Dressing Dip

This flavorful mixture can be used both as dip and salad dressing. Two or three spoonfuls are calorie free. Can be prepared ahead of time.

Mix in a small glass bowl:
   2/3 cup nonfat soy yogurt
   2 Tablespoons ketchup
   2 Tablespoons chopped green onion
   1 Tablespoon pickle relish
   1 Tablespoon chopped minced parsley
   1/4 teaspoon garlic salt

Serve with crisp carrot and celery sticks. Peel the carrots and remove the leaves from celery. Cut vegetables into 3 inch long narrow sticks and soak in ice water for 30 minutes to crisp. Drain and store in the refrigerator in a plastic bag until time to arrange around the dip.

Pink Party Spread

This tasty spread can be served with thin toasted slices of mini-bagels or with rounds of melba toast.

Combine in blender or processor:
   10.5 oz. package silken tofu
   2 Tablespoons soy yogurt
   2 Tablespoons onion juice
   1 teaspoon paprika

To get the onion juice, cut a raw onion in half and scrape the flat side. Taste dip and add salt as needed. Blend well, chill. *39 calories per tablespoon*

Apricot Ginger Dip

Make this several hours ahead so flavors mellow and fruits soften. Combine in a glass bowl:
2/3 cup low fat soy sour cream
1/3 cup low calorie eggless mayonnaise
2 Tablespoons crystallized ginger, chopped small
2 Tablespoons dried apricots, chopped small

Let dip chill several hours, stir once or twice. Just before serving, cut **3 large Granny Smith apples** into quarters, remove the seeds and slice each quarter into 6 thin pieces. Arrange half the apple slices around the dip. Sprinkle extra apple slices with the juice of a lemon and keep in a plastic bag to replenish the platter later. Rinse lemon juice off the stored slices before serving. *28 calories per tablespoon.*

Sparkly Cherry Tomatoes

These glisten in artificial light and look lovely on the table. Pick the small cherry tomatoes so they are bite-size.
1 pound small cherry tomatoes

Remove any stems from the tomatoes and rinse in cold water. Place wet tomatoes in a bowl and sprinkle with low sodium salt, shaking bowl so all the tomatoes are salted. Put bowl in refrigerator at once and chill several hours so the salt crystals harden. *8 calories per tomato.*

Carob Mint Cookies

Delicious little morsels to satisfy a sweet tooth. They are even better with the added crunch of toasted walnuts, hazelnuts or pecans but this is optional.

Prepare 2 cooky sheets by spraying lightly. Whisk together the dry ingredients:

3/4 cup unbleached flour
3/4 cup whole wheat pastry flour
1/2 cup carob powder
1/2 cup brown sugar, packed
1 teaspoon baking powder

Stir in the wet ingredients all at once:

1/2 cup applesauce
3 Tablespoons canola oil
2 Tablespoons water
1 teaspoon vanilla
1/2 teaspoon mint flavoring

If desired, add:

1/2 cup toasted walnuts, chopped

Preheat oven to 350 degrees. Drop mixture by the tablespoonful onto cooky sheets. Makes 30 cookies. Bake at 350 degrees about 10 minutes. Remove from sheet to cool. *42 calories per cooky.*

Helpful Hints for Holidays

If you are going out to an all evening party where there will be a lot of food and drinks, go with a friend who is interested in staying slim so you can give each other pep talks when drinks and tempting trays of food are passed. The wise dieter will drink seltzer or club soda with a twist of lemon or lime, or a spritzer with lots of ice, and make one drink last a long time. Beer and alcoholic drinks are loaded with calories.

At too many parties in the holiday season about the only thing that is okay to eat are the decorations on the appetizer tray, like the parsley sprigs, the carrot curls and the radish roses. But when you entertain at your house you are in control and can feature delectable food that is low in calories. This will delight everyone who is trying to stay slim as well as the lucky people who never gain a pound.

Index